Author Biographies

Maurice Sendak

Charlotte Guillain

www.raintreepublishers.co.uk
Visit our website to find out
more information about
Raintree books.

To order:
☎ Phone 0845 6044371
🖹 Fax +44 (0) 1865 312263
🖿 Email myorders@raintreepublishers.co.uk

Customers from outside the UK please telephone +44 1865 312262

Raintree is an imprint of Capstone Global Library Limited,
a company incorporated in England and Wales having its
registered office at 7 Pilgrim Street, London, EC4V 6LB
– Registered company number: 6695582

Text © Capstone Global Library Limited 2012
First published in hardback in 2012
The moral rights of the proprietor have been asserted.

Edited by Rebecca Rissman, Daniel Nunn,
  and Sian Smith
Designed by Joanna Hinton-Malivoire
Picture research by Tracy Cummins
Production by Victoria Fitzgerald
Originated by Capstone Global Library Ltd
Printed and bound in China by South China
  Printing Company Ltd

ISBN 978 1 406 23452 7
15 14 13 12 11
10 9 8 7 6 5 4 3 2 1

British Library Cataloguing in Publication Data
Guillain, Charlotte.
Maurice Sendak. – (Author biographies)   1.
Sendak, Maurice–Pictorial works–Juvenile literature. 2.
Authors, American–20th century–Biography–Pictorial works-
-Juvenile literature.
  I. Title II. Series
  813.5'4-dc22

Acknowledgements
We would like to thank the following for permission to
reproduce photographs: Alamy Images pp. 17, 23b (©
Illustration Works); AP Photo pp. 10, 23c (Susan Ragan), 20
(Mike Appleton); Corbis p. 11 (© Leon/Retna Ltd); Flickr
p. 8 (© Jim Lambert); Getty Images pp. 4 (David Corio/
Michael Ochs Archive), 5 (Spencer Platt/Getty Images),
9 (Robert Rosamilio/NY Daily News Archive), 12 (Jason
Kempin), 16 (Jupiterimages), 18 (Todd Plitt/Contour),
19, 23f (Carol Guzy/The Washington Post); The Kobal
Collection pp. 7 (RKO), 15, 21 (WARNER BROS); Library of
Congress Prints and Photographs Division p. 6; Rex USA p.
13 (PETER BROOKER); Shutterstock pp. 14 (© Mr. Arakelian),
23a (© discpicture), 23d (© shupian), 23e (© Falconia).

Cover photograph of Maurice Sendak standing by an
life-size scene from Where the Wild Things Are in 2002
reproduced with permission of Getty Images (James
Keyser/Time Life Pictures). Back cover images of a
Washington Ballet performance of 'Where the Wild Things
Are' in 2007 reproduced with permission of Getty Images
(Carol Guzy/The Washington Post).

Every effort has been made to contact copyright holders
of material reproduced in this book. Any omissions will be
rectified in subsequent printings if notice is given to the
publisher.

Contents

Some words are shown in bold, **like this**. You can find them in the glossary on page 23.

Who is Maurice Sendak?

Maurice Sendak is a writer.

He writes and draws the pictures for children's books.

Children all over the world love Maurice Sendak's books.

His most famous book is *Where The Wild Things Are*.

Where did he grow up?

Maurice Sendak was born in 1928.

He grew up in New York in the United States.

When he was a child, he was often ill and spent a lot of time reading books.

He loved to watch cartoons and films, such as *King Kong*.

What did he do before he was a writer?

Maurice loved drawing when he was young.

He went to art school to study at night.

He also worked in a toy shop, putting displays in the windows.

He worked and studied hard for four years.

How did he start writing books?

Maurice started drawing pictures for other people's books.

He started to become famous as an **illustrator**.

In 1963 he wrote and drew the pictures for *Where The Wild Things Are*.

This book made him famous all over the world.

What books has he written?

After *Where The Wild Things Are*, Maurice wrote many other books.

Higglety Pigglety Pop is about a dog who goes looking for adventure.

In The Night Kitchen describes a boy's adventures in a strange dreamworld.

Outside Over There is about a girl who rescues her baby sister from goblins.

What does he write about?

Maurice's stories are often about dark and scary places and things.

His stories often happen at night when things are spooky and different.

Many of his stories are about brave children and other heroes.

They travel to other worlds and stand up to things that scare them.

How does Maurice Sendak draw his pictures?

Some of Maurice Sendak's pictures are black and white.

Many **illustrators** draw pictures with pen and ink.

Maurice often uses a style called **cross-hatching**.

This is when lots of lines cross over each other.

What else does he like to do?

Maurice has a home in the countryside and a flat in New York City.

He loves spending time with his dog, called Herman.

Maurice is also interested in the theatre.

He has made costumes and **stage sets** for ballets and **operas**.

Why is he famous today?

People all over the world buy Maurice Sendak's books.

He has won many **awards**, including the Caldecott Medal for *Where The Wild Things Are*.

A film of *Where The Wild Things Are* was made in 2009.

People have also performed an **opera** of the story.

Timeline of Maurice Sendak's life and work

1928   Maurice Sendak was born in Brooklyn, New York.

1948   He started working in a toy shop.

1963   *Where The Wild Things Are* was **published**.

1981   *Outside Over There* was published.

2009   A film of *Where The Wild Things Are* was made.

Glossary

award a prize

cross-hatching style of drawing where lines cross each other closely

illustrator person who draws or paints pictures to go with a story

opera a play that is set to music

published made into a book and printed

stage set the scenery in the background on a theatre stage

Find out more

Books

Some of Maurice Sendak's books: *Where The Wild Things Are, Higglety Pigglety Pop, In The Night Kitchen,* and *Outside Over There.*

Maurice Sendak (First Biographies), Eric Braun (Capstone, 2005)

Maurice Sendak (My Favourite Writer), Jennifer Hurtig (Weigl Publishers, 2006)

Maurice Sendak (Who Wrote That?), Hal Marcovitz (Chelsea House, 2006)

Websites

http://www.harpercollinschildrens.com/Kids/ AuthorsAndIllustrators/ContributorDetail. aspx?Cld=12708
Visit the Harper Collins website to learn more about Maurice Sendak and see inside some of his books.

Index